Be
Coachable

Tools and Tips from a
Top Executive Coach

JILL CHIAPPE

Dedication

This book is humbly dedicated to my parents,
the two people who made me who I am today.
My parents are kind, loving, helpful people,
the kind of people any of us would want as parents.

Contents

Acknowledgments

My deepest appreciation to my husband Tim who encouraged me to write this book and gave numerous ideas and endless support for my writing. To my children who patiently suffered through having no mother temporarily while I was consumed with work. And to all of my clients who encouraged me to write down some of the ideas I taught them to use.

And, finally, to all those who want to be more successful.

You are the glue that holds our country together.

Introduction

Jeff, the VP of Product for a Fortune 500 company, stood outside the conference room door and broke into a cold sweat. He reached for the door knob but did not turn it. He stood still for a few seconds, running through his presentation in his mind. He was proposing a massive pivot for the product strategy and the VP of Engineering might lose his mind as soon as he saw that slide.

At that moment, he sent me a text:

"Standing outside conference room. Can't go in."

"Ok. Don't go in," I replied.

"Have to," buzzed back.

"Nah, you don't need a job," I retorted.

"Ha ha. My mortgage is killing me."

"Then I guess you should go in," I conceded.

"Ok, but if they throw me out, you owe me a million dollars."

"I'll take the bet."

I chuckled as I sent the final text. My phone was quiet so I assumed he opened the door after that.

I had worked with Jeff for several months on his product strategy and how he would present it at the leadership team meeting that day. He had prepped his colleagues as much as possible for this day and had his brightest team member polish the presentation. The rest was up to him.

I found out a day later that Jeff's presentation went smoothly. The team accepted the pivot which resulted in a growth to the company of 16% over the following year. Needless to say, it was a win-win.

You will never hear my name in conjunction with this success. You would never even know I was involved unless you knew

"Jeff" personally. But I was involved, and Jeff sent me an email the following day that said, "Thank you for your support. You were pivotal in helping me survive the stress and strain of this huge change of direction for us. Your advice on how to approach the other executives was invaluable." Moments like that make my job worthwhile.

The truth is, executive coaching is a bit of an underground profession. Many clients tell me the most important thing I can do for them is never mention that I even know them. You won't see any real names in this book, or any actual client stories here either. Jeff's story has his name and all the relevant details changed. Why? Because some of the most important and influential people in the business world today have called on an executive coach and they don't want you to know about it. It's better if you assume that they were born into the world with all the brilliance and skill worthy of a c-level executive. And the fact that they needed some help along the way is just between you and me. *Wink, wink.*

But that does not mean I want to keep my secrets from you. Many of the tricks and tips that these executives needed to survive in the world of business are helpful to you and they are included in this book. I hope you fare as well with it as they have. To your success!

Section I:
Setting the Scene

Definitions

———◆———

If you would converse with me, you must define your terms.

—VOLTAIRE

360° review: feedback that comes from all around an employee. Feedback is provided by direct reports, peers, and supervisors. It may be contrasted with traditional performance appraisal where the employee is most often reviewed only by the manager. It is called a 360° review because it takes feedback from 360° around the executive or manager.

Coachee: The one being coached. The client who hires a coach or consults with a coach.

Coach: One who guides and leads through instruction, demonstration and practice.

Executive: One who executes; one who gets things done in a business. Usually responsible for a large area of the business and holding a title of Vice President or above.

Manager: One who manages a team or group of people. Usually responsible for a smaller area than an executive and usually a direct report of the executive. May hold titles like Director, Manager or Team Lead.

This book applies equally to managers and executives, and the research included hundreds of executives and managers in many industries. For the purposes of this book, the words manager and executive are used interchangeably to indicate that the types of skills are similar in content, if not in scope.

What is executive coaching?

———◆———

What is Executive Coaching?

"A good coach is someone who can give correction without causing resentment."
--JOHN WOODEN

A vast majority of the clients or potential clients I meet initially have no idea what executive coaching means or how it works. They may not even know what the word *coach* itself means and they may conjure up images of a football coach, a yelling personal trainer, a life coach or a dozen other inaccurate pictures.

100% of Olympic athletes have a coach. Why shouldn't a top-paid executive?

In sports, a coach is a person who leads and guides a team through instruction, demonstration and intense practice. The sports coach definition is workable for executive coaching with a slight modification. The job of the executive coach is to use examples, demonstration, instruction and best practices to help an executive do his best job. Intense practice is occasionally a component. The keynote of good coaching is **improvement of skills**. A coach must get results! The one caveat is that coaches are not always hired to improve *business* results. At times, the executive already does excellent work but has a hard time working in a team or getting along with others. In those cases, the coach works with the person to ensure that those good results are not lost among poor team relationships or annoyed colleagues. The coach may seek improvement in interpersonal relationships in this case.

How are coaches and consultants different?

An executive coach is not the same as a consultant. The executive coach can and will give advice at times, but that is not the primary role of a coach. The coach uses training, discussion, practical examples and exercises to help the person see the answers for herself. If you want an opinion on an action to take in a specialized area, such as social media marketing, an executive coach may not be the right choice. If you want someone to teach you the skills needed take your executive performance to the next level, a coach is definitely the right choice. The chart below shows the differences between coaches and consultants:

Coach	Consultant
Suggests changes to best practices as learned through experience and observation	Will do individual contributor work as well as giving advice
Broad role, covering all executive competencies	Specific role and focus, e.g. social media consultant
Works with one person at a time, with occasional group education sessions	Works independently, in teams or one-on-one
Helps an executive "learn to fish", teaching the skills or competencies necessary for the executive to learn her own way	"Fishes" for the company, acts as extended workforce for the company
Operates in conjunction with the executive	Operates independently, but gives advice
Strategic focus on goals, aspirations, confidence, competency and personal fulfillment for the executive	Tactical focus on area for which he is hired, e.g, customer retention

Clearly, the coach and consultant roles will at times overlap, but the main functions of a coach should be separate and distinct. A competent executive coach uses the following guidelines.

1. **Coach toward improvement**. The job of a coach is to create improvement in the executive. The areas of improvement depend on what the coach was hired to do, and so a good beginning is clearly important. Have the executive write his or her goals down clearly. Take those goals and determine a way they could be measured. Then use that measurement as a guide to see improvement. When the coach sets up a program for the executive, all assignments should be aimed at improving the area of the goal, even if slightly.

2. **Coach one skill at a time.** The executive may have 17 goals. Pick one, or two at the outside, to begin your work. Work on that until the improvement is satisfactory. Then go to the next development area and do the same. Get improvement a bit at a time, not all at once. Don't expect the person to go from zero to perfect in one session. Change is more long-lasting if it takes place step-by-step, at a reasonable pace and over time, continually improving toward a goal. This is not a justification for going slowly, but a method of making the change stick.

3. **Coach realistically.** When helping the executive to acquire a skill, such as delegation, use examples that are realistic and relate to the situation at hand. Be creative, but within the realm of actual experience. As much as possible, try to understand the unique aspects of his or her role, industry and organization and coach to that unique reality.

4. **Coach with care.** Although nearly every coach can follow a certain protocol, or use a formula, not every coach can truly care about his coachee. Without actual care and concern, the coach won't get very far in creating change. Spend some time getting to the point where you, the coach, are ready and willing to coach the executive. Don't begin coaching until you are sure you can care about the person enough to help.

Preparing for a Coaching Relationship

Whether you are an HR professional, a peer, a mentor or a coach, you need basic tools to begin to assist another person. If you are an executive and simply want to coach your direct reports to improve their performance, the same rules apply. Use these principles to get any coaching or mentoring relationship off the starting block.

Improvement

As irrational as it may sound, not every person who seeks coaching wants to improve his situation. Some are trying to get out of a role or the company and just want to be coached as to how to do this. Others have a solemn belief that no improvement is possible, that "people are the way they are". If you do not quickly understand this about your coachee, you may end up at odds because you intend improvement while he intends to leave or go through the motions of a fruitless exercise. Nothing is more important than setting up the relationship with aligned purposes. To begin, ask your coachee his goals for coaching by finding out what end state he desires. Then, pull off any false veneer of "playing along" with coaching by asking the questions below:

1. Is there anything about your current role that you do not like? If so, what?
2. What area of your job causes you the most stress?
3. If you could leave to go do anything else, what would you do?
4. Is there anything about your role which makes you feel old or tired?
5. Is there any reason why you would want to give up?
6. Do you believe people can change for the better? Have you ever seen someone improve in any area? What was it?

Get several answers for each of the above questions. These questions are food for a discussion, and are not intended for short 'yes' or 'no' answers. If the person mentions any fact or situation which is fascinating, confusing or worth discussing, ask further about it until it is perfectly clear. Take the role of detective in understanding the situation and goals of your coachee. When you are certain he would like improvement, not to leave or follow some other purpose, continue with the next section.

Help Me?

Clearly, a main role of the coach is to help the executive, to be a sounding board, a stable source of guidance and a font of wisdom. But not everyone is open to accepting help from a coach. This is easy to understand for those who have been to a dentist or a doctor and had a painful experience. We go in to the doctor, relieved to get help for our illness or our toothache, and end up with a needle in our backside or our jaw, followed by a painful procedure or two, and some follow-up medication. As helpful the intervention is in solving the condition, it never sets us up to love the idea of help. Years later, we see people avoiding the doctor even when a condition has become serious. We can get the idea that help involves a little bit, or a great deal, of pain.

This is the view on help that you might find your coachee (or even yourself) sitting in.

Thus, the job of a coach is to get the coachee ready and willing to receive the help of a coach. Poke around about his reactions to help. Ask the following questions to start discussion:

1. What types of help has he or she received before?
2. Was any of the help bad help? Any good help? What happened?
3. What does help consist of in his mind?
4. Has he ever been coached before? How did it go? Was the coach helpful?
5. Who has helped him most in life? Least?
6. Describe the ideal type of help.

This is also a good time to check for experiences similar to coaching but not called "coaching", such as having a mentor. Ask the following questions and get complete answers:

1. Has the person had a mentor? Used a consultant? Anything similar to a coach? If yes to any, find out whether this helped or not.
2. What types of experiences does he or she associate with coaching? Were those good experiences or bad experiences?
3. Does he believe coaching could work? Is it possible that it could help?
4. Give an example of how coaching **might** help someone. Give an example of when you have seen someone receive help.

Please note, this set of questions could take as long as several hours, but minimally will take about 30 - 45 minutes. After digging in deeply to find the answers to these questions, and if the person is ready and willing to receive some help, move into the next step on control. If this *Help* portion is rocky or left unfinished, refer to the next section entitled *Coachability.*

Coachability

Not Everyone Is Coachable

Although help may seem to be an innocuous subject, it is actually a powderkeg. When you question a person about help, any of a variety of reactions can occur, from grief and tears to anger and shouting. The person may feel embarrassed to talk about help with you. He may leave the room and never come back, saying it is "too personal". As a coach, you have to be brave and face up to whatever reactions the person may have to help as a subject. Get through all the questions in the *Help Me* section. If the person leaves at this point and refuses coaching, do not be discouraged. A person who cannot receive help cannot be coached, so your efforts would have been fruitless anyway. Find another person to coach who can get through this step.

Having a sane reaction to help is the make-or-break point of a coaching relationship. Help is the primer coat on the canvas of coaching. With a belief in help, a beautiful outcome is possible. Without it, uneven and unpredictable results may occur. A key point is never to assume that others have the same view on help that you have. They do not. You must ask the questions and find where the person truly stands by hearing it directly from him or her.

There is also another barrier to coachability. It has to do with the person's own sense of integrity. Have you noticed how some people never seem to improve despite how many classes they go to? Or how many performance reviews they weather? Sometimes the person even cheerfully attends seminars but never changes behavior. He gives coaching, training and even HR a bad name.

Does the following scenario sound familiar? At the office birthday party, the crowd avoids one person continually. He might be the office gossip, the aloof engineer, or the one who steals others' ideas and passes them off as his own. Either way, he is trouble. As he exits his yearly performance review, the whole office watches carefully, hoping he has somehow come out a changed man. Over and over, his colleagues are disappointed. Why is that?

A basic concept of coaching is that a person develops certain habits or patterns that he truly believes help him to survive in the workplace. Those patterns are engrained because at some point, they worked.

> **Example**: James steals some presentation data from a co-worker and gives the best presentation of his life. He gets promoted as a result. Now, he has found a perfect reason to keep stealing data. He justifies to himself and others why stealing the data was acceptable and convinces himself enough to make it a blind spot. Four or five jobs later, he is still stealing others' ideas even though it no longer works and others shun him. It is obvious to everyone around him this is a problem, but he is oblivious. This is an ethical problem for him created by an earlier successful action. Even worse, because it is now a thoroughly justified blind spot, he is not even aware that he needs to change this behavior. What is obvious to his colleagues is a hidden problem for him.

What can we do for this workplace problem child? How can we help him?

Remember: In the absence of ethical behavior, no improvement will occur.

Ethical problems shut off the ability to learn. The person, to keep his blind spots about his unethical behavior, has to develop blind spots in related areas. So if you have your eye on someone who "just doesn't get it", is not self-aware, or never changes, you have your eyes on someone who needs an ethics tune-up. He just is not coachable yet.

The pyramid below shows the relationship between ethics and learning or professional development.

A strong ethical foundation allows for skill building and professional development. A person who has to lead others cannot do so unless he has others' best interests in mind. *A person who has ethical trouble thinks mainly about himself and that pits him against everyone else.* He also develops blind spots because of the mechanism of hiding from himself that his unethical "successful action" is wrong. The easiest way to spot an ethics problem is to look for long-standing blind spots or places where the person simply cannot learn or improve. His level of ethics is what you are actually complaining about when you complain he "doesn't get it".

The good news is that ethical troubles can be fixed. But please do not waste your time trying to coach a leader when his ethics are messy. Handle the ethical problems first. If you have trouble with where to start to create ethical stability, or if the problems are too deep-rooted and your courage is flagging, call on a professional coach or HR person who can dig in deep and get the ethical problems fixed. Then, when the person is truly ready, give him a development plan that will allow him to soar.

Control

———◆———

Assuming you now have a person who is interested in help and whose ethics are acceptable, the next step in developing a coaching relationship is to come to an agreement about who is in control in the coaching relationship. Control is another dirty word in the workplace, second only to help. Sit any person down and tell him you are going to control him and he will likely leap from the chair and run from the room, possibly screaming. And yet, to have a successful coaching relationship, someone has to control the flow of the development plan, and the most likely candidate is the coach, not the coachee. So to have a successful relationship, a coach must help his coachee come to terms with the fact that the coach will control him and the process.

To get the subject of control patched up, the coach can ask the coachee the following questions:

1. When you hear "control" what do you think of?

2. Have you had any bad experiences with control? What happened?

3. Have you had a good experience with control?

4. How do you like to be controlled?

5. How do you dislike being controlled?

6. Is control ever a good thing? Give an example.

Next, spend a few minutes asking the coachee to do various tasks, such as hand over his pen, get up from his chair, or bring you a glass of water. They should be simple tasks, but he should be willing to do them with no questions asked. Some executives balk at this. Even an individual contributor might balk. Don't worry, just proceed with the questions and dig in deeper. Getting a person to agree to do these simple tasks is a minimum threshold for control to start a coaching relationship.

The control exercises are similar to the ones on help. They should take a minimum of 30 - 45 minutes and could go as long as several hours. Dig deeply to find areas where the person was controlled badly or the control was harmful. These experiences are likely to get in the way of coaching unless you uncover them and bring them to light.

If you manage to dig in deep enough, you will get to a point where the coachee trusts you to control him, knowing that control can be a positive influence. After all, if you were operating your phone and didn't control it, you wouldn't make many calls, would you? You would likely end up with a broken phone. You can mention this to your coachee to make a point about control.

Goals

Surely you have heard the old adage that if you don't know where you are going, any road will do. If coaching is a path, it has to have an end point, a place to arrive. That place is a goal. Feel free to set as many goals as you like with your coachee, but remember the admonition in the introduction about coaching only *one item at a time*.

Goal setting is important to achieve focus. The literature on goal-setting is vast and worth reading. For further information on goal-setting, read any literature regarding "SMART goals". In actuality, setting goals is very natural to a human being, so your coachee may have come in with several goals already in mind. As an added complexity, your coachee may have several goals handed down to him by his boss or even the HR partner. Your job is to sort through these goals and find the first goal which will not only achieve improvement for your coachee, but one which you can gain the willingness of the coachee to pursue. **Without willingness, coaching is impossible.**

When the coachee brings his list of goals, the key for you as a coach is to:

1. narrow these goals to achievable size and write them down;

2. to choose the priority goals among the list of goals;

3. to clarify the path to the chosen goal; and

4. to apply the appropriate tools on the path to the goal.

A word of warning about goals: Do not accept goals which are foisted upon the coachee and which he is not willing to pursue. You will waste a tremendous amount of time. If you are unsure if your coachee is willing to pursue a goal, ask the questions in the help section specifically related to that goal. If he feels help is possible on this goal, you can also pursue coaching.

If your coachee has no idea where to begin with goals, consider doing a self-directed performance review or 360°. This can be done professionally with a company that performs 360s or can be done informally by the person himself, perhaps assisted by the Human Resources partner. *More information on this process is found in the "Tools" section.*

Now the real work begins. You have worked with your executive or employee to get him ready to receive coaching and you have documented a goal to begin work on. Take the goal you chose to begin coaching and find the chapter that is most suitable for working on that goal. If you do not know which chapter applies, feel free to read them all for inspiration.

Section II:
Tools

Performance Evaluation

—————◆—————

The vast majority of executives and managers begin every year with a new performance evaluation. For those who do not have this process in place, it can be helpful to begin a coaching engagement with a baseline of this type. To do a brief version of the performance review, see the guidelines below.

No Recent Performance Evaluation?

If you need to create a performance evaluation from scratch, take the person's job description and break it down into categories. Try not to list more than 12 or 15 competency areas at the outside. If you have no job description available, search the job title on the internet with the words "job description" included, e.g., "VP of Marketing job description". Pull out the parts that apply to the role and break it down into categories. Be sure to include soft skills such as influence or conflict management as relevant.

Consider the purpose of the role and clear that up directly with the coachee. Be certain this is written and that the goals, abilities and competencies match up with this purpose and are prioritized accordingly. For example, if the person's role is CFO, the purpose of the role would be to manage the financial aspects of the organization to enhance profitability and viability. With that in mind, some of the top technical skills might be financial acumen and experience with mergers and acquisitions. Some of the top soft skills might be negotiation, results focus and detail-orientation. These prioritizations would be completely different for other types of roles. Use your common sense or get an HR representative or coach to help if needed.

Next, have the person do a self-assessment on the competencies and skills you prioritized. Then include as many people as realistic in evaluating the person in the time allotted. The people to include can be the manager, peers, direct reports or any other stakeholders that know the person well. A simple evaluation can include a rating scale and a box for comments. A more complicated one can include a rating scale and associated questions. A simple 360° process can be purchased at a reasonable price through our website at www.becoachable.com/services/360-leadership/.

Competencies

The most common areas of improvement for executives are listed in the following table by frequency. These percentages were gathered from the hundreds of executive 360's we have performed over the last decade in our company and in partnership with other companies.

If an executive had more negative comments than positive comments in an area, it is considered a "development area" for the purposes of a 360° review. These development areas show common themes and they are listed in the table by frequency of appearance.

Graphic 2

Development Area	Percentage of Executives Requiring Coaching in this Area
Onboarding	12% / 88%*
Results Focus	62%
Problem-Solving	58%
Interpersonal Skills	58%
Delegation	44%
Influence	32%
Communication	31%
Executive Presence	22%

While Onboarding was only a development area in 12% total of the reports we performed, of those who had recently begun a new role, 88% needed onboarding help in their development plans.

Tools for improving these top areas of development are include in the next section. Additionally, an example set of 360 review questions follows.

Example 360° Review Questions

———◆———

N ote: *These questions were designed for executive reviews, but can be modified to work for managers or even individual contributors. The idea is to look at competencies that are required for the role and ask questions which get to the heart of those competencies. Be certain to change the pronouns and add the company name where appropriate.*

For a soft copy of this list of questions, email us at admin@becoachable. com.

1. **Overall Leadership and Management**:

   a. Main strengths in her leadership and management?

   b. Main development areas?

2. **Onboarding** (if recently hired or in new role):

   a. Did she effectively transition into her new role?

   b. Has she grasped the most important parts of her role?

c. Any major failures or missing actions in her role?

d. Anything she is doing particularly well?

3. **Results Focus:**

    a. Does she get results?

    b. What problems does she encounter in getting results?

    c. Is she creative in solving these problems?

    d. Does she make excuses for not getting results?

4. **Interpersonal Relationships:**

    a. Is she approachable?

    b. How would you describe her communication style?

    c. What type of atmosphere does her communication create?

    d. Does she connect with her team members at a personal and professional level?

    e. Does she convey difficult information diplomatically?

5. **Delegation & Empowerment:**

    a. Does she delegate too much? Not enough?

    b. When she delegates, does she also empower?

    c. Any micromanagement? If so, on what types of issues?

    d. Does she tend to over-control decisions?

e. Is she involved in too many decisions or projects? If so, where?

6. **Influence:**

   a. Is she able to influence others? Why or why not?

   b. Is she persuasive? Persistent?

   c. Does she hold her position firmly or waver?

7. **Strategic Thinking**:

   a. Are you aware of her overall strategy for her area?

   b. How well has she communicated this?

   c. Do you know how your daily work relates to the strategy?

   d. Is the strategy innovative?

8. **Business Acumen**:

   a. Describe her overall business acumen (knowledge and ability)?

   b. Does she operate at the right level? If no, is she too tactical or too high level?

   c. Is she knowledgeable about business operations and strategy?

9. **[Departmental] Acumen** (fill in name of appropriate department):

   a. Does she know her area [Finance, Technology, Sales, etc.] well?

b. Is she well-versed in the tools that streamline this area?

c. Any areas of [department] where she is particularly strong? Particularly weak?

10. **Openness to Learning:**

a. Does she accept new ideas?

b. Does she listen to opposing viewpoints?

c. Does she integrate new ideas and ways of doing things?

11. **Teambuilding:**

a. How well does she build collaborative teams?

b. Does she hire good team players?

c. Does she encourage team work or pit teammates against each other?

d. Has she failed to hire any key players?

12. **Planning & Execution**:

a. Does she have a plan or set of project plans for her direct reports?

b. Are plans easy to understand and follow daily?

c. Do the plans align with the vision and strategy?

d. Do all parts of the department easily coordinate?

13. Executive Presence:

a. How well does she present to the leadership team? Her manager? In other settings?

b. Does she show composure and maturity in her interactions?

c. Does she take courageous stances?

14. Cultural Creation:

a. What kind of culture has she created in her department?

b. Any dysfunctional parts of the culture? If so, what are they?

15. Organizational Development:

a. Is she thoughtful about how the organization is designed for future success?

b. Does she create and clarify roles which forward the business purposes?

c. Is she creating an organization which serves the needs of the business?

d. Are any roles unclear or missing?

16. Recruiting/Hiring:

a. How does she do at presenting the company well?

b. Do people want to come work for her?

c. Does she expand her team continually?

d. Does she find great candidates to work for her?

e. Is there solid succession planning?

17. **Coaching & Performance Management:**

a. Does she help team members grow and develop?

b. Does she give stretch assignments?

c. Does she give relevant, actionable feedback?

d. Do her team members feel they can grow with the company?

18. **Problem Solving & Decision-Making:**

a. How does she make decisions? Analytically? Emotionally?

b. Does she make decisions and then change course?

c. Does she make decisions others can understand?

d. How are decisions conveyed?

e. Do decisions stick or do they change often?

19. **Other:**

a. What else would you like to say?

b. Any areas we missed?

c. What would help us to get the full picture of her leadership?

OnBoarding

---

*Onboarding = the process of entering a new role and getting up to speed.

One of the trickiest executive skills to learn is how to onboard effectively. Why? For most executives, egos get in the way. Many executives or new employees make the mistake of thinking they know all about the new role before they arrive in it. If you have ever seen a business fail because it sold a product no one wanted, you are witnessing similar effects to poor onboarding. Onboard correctly and you integrate smoothly. Fail to do so and you will soon be sending out resumes again.

When you arrive newly into an organization or a role, you are **unknown** in that area. No matter how effective, famous, diligent or brilliant you were in your former role, you are now a zero. Don't be offended. Just onboard correctly. Below are the steps to a successful onboarding.

Review your predecessor's actions. Who was in the role before you? Was he or she successful? If so, draw up a list of what he did that made him successful. If not, congratulations. You have a blank slate.

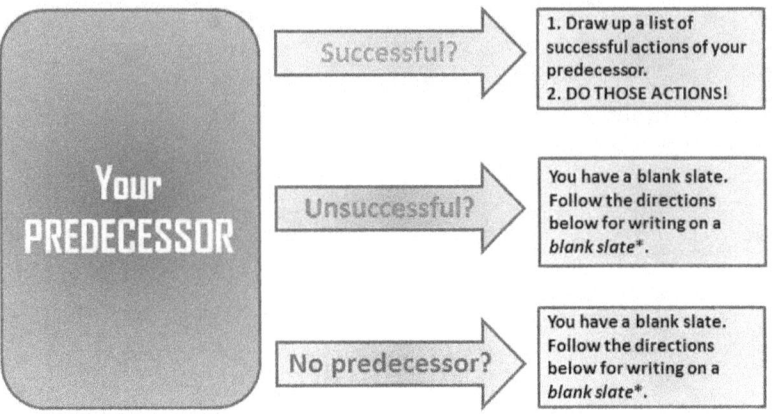

Writing on a Blank Slate*.

a. If you have to construct your role with no information from your predecessor, begin with an intelligent approach to data gathering. First of all, know where you fit into the organization. Find yourself on the org chart.

b. Who are all the key players, influencers and stakeholders? Ask around to see who has the most impact on your team. Draw up a list of those above, below and laterally who will influence you. This list should include any person with whom you regularly interact or from whom you need important data. Potential people for your list: your manager (if any), anyone else in your department, the key cross-functional contacts, Board members, clients or customers.

c. Seek these people out and first tell them a brief "elevator pitch" about yourself. Next, start asking questions. *Remember you have between 30 - 90 days to complete this step once you are in role. After that time, your questions become a sign of weakness.

Questions to ask:

a. How do you see my role?

b. Anything I should be doing? Anything I should avoid doing?

c. What does success look like for me?

d. What is the worst thing I could do in my role?

e. How can I help you in your role?

f. What types of information do you expect to receive from me?

g. What deliverables would you expect me to produce?

---

d. The final step is to craft a description of your role from your data. Write it down as concisely as possible and plan out how you can do it.

e. Then, execute! As a quick final note, you might want to let the stakeholders know when you have begun executing. Make it known that you did what they asked you to do. This closes the loop of communication with the stakeholders. It is also good relationship-building for you.

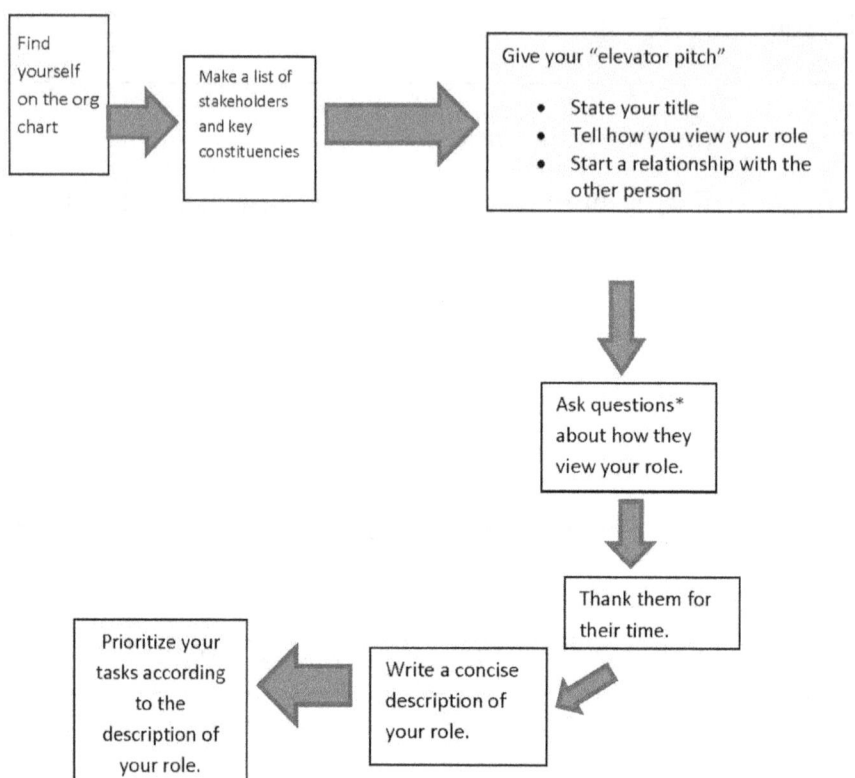

A key point to remember when onboarding is that every stakeholder may have a different view of your role. I discovered this once while asking about a marketing person I was coaching during the onboarding process. As we asked around about the role, the priorities that each person listed were so vastly different that she could have held three different roles. At that point, we had to prioritize and refine the role before going back to each person with a finalized version of what the role truly meant and what it didn't mean. After she got agreement on the refined role, she was able to start executing with certainty.

Key point: Onboarding is successful when productivity is evident in the area. If confusion, low morale or low productivity occur, re-check the onboarding steps.

Results Focus

No Excuses EVER

What IS the most important characteristic of a leader? You may have heard many answers such as: character, strength, a genius IQ. While these are all helpful, our research led us to this answer: no excuses. The technical term for this might be "accountability" or "responsibility" but we like "no excuses" because it conveys the real, raw truth of the matter.

The real, raw truth is that a fantastic executive is able to make things happen and she never makes excuses when she can't do it.

Take the stories of these two real-life executives. One, the CEO of a technology start-up, ran into trouble with her company. The idea of her company was a unique and ingenious one, but she just couldn't get any traction in the market. A fantastic executive herself, she ordered an immediate review of herself, with interviews from all of her investors and a harsh but truthful look at her executive skills. She found several deficiencies in herself such as a weak financial background and some difficulties in PR and marketing. She instantly hired a consultant to help her with her PR and marketing, and she found a part-time CFO to fill in her financial gap. She started really kicking the market in the teeth and got on the cover of a major magazine.

Another CEO, head of a $35 million technology company that was in the transition phase from startup to mid-size found himself losing the buy-in of his executive team. He lost his VP of Sales and his Chief Engineer before he called us. Then, when we arrived, he went on and on for hours about how the problem was the founder of the business. The only problem with his excuse was that the founder had been around long before the exodus had begun. It just didn't add up. This CEO was completely unable to look at his own contribution to the recent problems.

The difference between these two types of leaders is a simple one. The first CEO was a no excuses CEO! She was able to face up to her weaknesses and charge ahead with solutions, unfazed by any critical or difficult feedback she might have gotten. The success of the company was more important to her than her personal pride. The other CEO, unfortunately, was so involved in finding who to blame that he couldn't even see beyond his own nose.

A "no excuses" executive does not judge his company or his team by whether everything is perfect. That is wrong standard. The question is whether he can look at his company or team and, despite everything that is wrong, still make things turn out right. In the process, such an executive might even find that he or she has much to learn or many changes to make before all is well. Despite these difficulties, a no excuses executive charges ahead.

If you aren't sure if you are a "no excuses" leader, take this short quiz:

QUIZ

1. When something goes wrong, do you usually search for who is to blame?

2. Do you look at the day ahead and see only problems?

3. Do positive people annoy you?

4. Do you wonder why everyone around you is so much dumber or lazier than you?

5. Do you blame any recent career or job failures on the "bad economy"?

If you answered "yes" to more than three of these questions, you are having a tough time being a "no excuses" leader. You may need to take a longer leadership assessment test to determine why you have a tough time taking responsibility.

We are the first to admit that being a "no excuses" leader is not easy. On rough days or around tax time, we all might wish for a good scapegoat. The hard, unfriendly truth of the matter is that those who have the most success are the ones who can look at any situation and determine how they caused it.

So if you are looking at a financial disaster in your company, or a human resources nightmare, or any of the myriad problems that can occur, pull yourself up by the bootstraps and consider this:

1. Just because you are "no excuses" does not mean you should engage in self-pity or blame. Just acknowledge the situation and get moving on a solution.

2. A good analysis of how the problem occurred goes a long way toward solving it. If you can't figure it out, get a professional in the area to help you.

3. Don't get distracted. Just because something is unpleasant does not mean you should avoid it. It's always better to attack a problem than avoid it.

4. There's nothing better than getting it DONE. So take that hairy problem and handle it.

Finally, take heart in this brilliant quote from Thomas Edison: "We are continually faced by great opportunities brilliantly disguised as insoluble problems."

Key point: Results alone make or break a leader.

Problem-Solving

A good executive makes good decisions.

The concept seems simple. However, with so many people and so many variables, an executive can get lost in how to make decisions efficiently.

Start with the definition of a problem. A problem consists mainly of opposed forces.

A doubt or anxiety will occur when those opposed forces are roughly equivalent. So the best method to solve any problem is to write down what the opposed forces are, starting with your own thoughts. This is a solo exercise for the moment.

Example: You want to hire a new project manager but are unsure whether it is a good use of your team's resources.

Make a list of pros and cons by drawing a line down the center of a paper. Now, on the pros side (left), list for yourself all the benefits to having a project manager. On the right, list all the cons.

IMPORTANT: As you do so, be certain to write any past decisions not to have a project manager or any past bad experiences with a project manager. You may cross these off later if you decide they are not relevant to the current problem. But do not fail to write them down because they are currently influencing your thought on the matter. As you write the cons, you may notice that you have unearthed some new pros. Write those down as well.

A main idea in this exercise is to determine what the most important parts of the role will be based on what you truly need, and to remove any doubt you may have based on old, irrelevant experiences. The way an executive gets into trouble in his thinking is by applying old generalities, such as "all outside consultants are bad" or "project managers are lazy". If you have any thoughts like these, be sure to write them down so they can be removed from the list as known, irrelevant items. This pro/con list is only for your own use unless you decide to share it.

When you feel you have a good decision in place based on the pros and cons, you may realize that you will have to influence others to agree with your decision. This is covered further in the section on influence. All good decisions start with certainty. So gain this first.

Key point: Good decisions start with your own certainty.

Interpersonal Skills

Part One

———◆———

Judging Character

Every decision in your company involves people in some way, whether it involves people to execute it or people to buy into it. And yet, so many people have trouble dealing with even the slightest difficulty in interpersonal relationships. This is a vast subject, and will not be covered comprehensively here, but will touch on a few key points that will assist you in hiring, influencing and working in teams.

Think of a goal you achieved without the assistance of other people. Can't think of anything? The fact is, we need other people to help us accomplish goals. But how do we know who will help us and who will slow us down along the way?

A teacher I knew used to philosophize that there were only two types of people in the world: good guys and bad guys. While this may have been true, it left me with no tools to sort out which was which. For instance, were my business competitors all "bad guys" or might some of them be "good guys"? I needed a practical and workable system for determining whether someone was on my side or not, whether I could trust them or not. I finally found that one method worked best to answer these questions about people.

First of all, I stopped listening to what people were saying. Some of the most underhanded people I ever worked with said wonderful, flattering words to my face and then proceeded to undermine me relentlessly. So words were not the test of whether a person could be trusted. I needed a better system. What I discovered was that I could look for business results and get a good estimation of the worth of the person. I started dividing people into two camps. Rather than "good" or "bad", which had too many extraneous connotations, I started using "constructive" and "destructive". Either a person was helping me and the business or he wasn't. Either he was pushing for results for the team or he wasn't. This made the picture much clearer. I also found that the minute I focused on results and those who were constructive in achieving them or destructive of them, I could easily sort out a few other "types" in each camp.

Below are the "types" found most commonly, with genders chosen randomly for each type. The types are meant to characterize broad groups of people and are not fully complete but contain subtleties. These characters are only useful to determine if a person is someone you might want on your team.

THE CONSTRUCTIVE TYPES: These types get results for self. They help others get results.

1. **Busy**: Rather than being a busy-body, he is just plain busy. Phone calls, emails, meetings—he goes all day long. He is just busy, busy, busy getting things done! He does not just do busy-work, mind you. He is closing loops and

completing work. This is the top person to have on a team that wants to achieve results.

2. **Hero:** He is the ultra-constructive hero of the office. He likes to pitch in, works hard and goes a tad nutty when others try to stop him. If he complains, it is about injustices or the barriers to success. On a normal day, he is busy and optimistic. He likes to talk and may even run late from getting too involved in some conversations. He loves having an exciting goal to pursue and likes other people a great deal.

3. **Thoughtful**: She is concerned about the results, thoroughly thinking through strategies and timelines. She ponders about data and furrows her brow at complex problems. Likes to review charts and spreadsheets. New ideas are a bit too risky because they might jeopardize the cause. She's helpful and a good person to go to for a thorough analysis.

4. **Blah**: He's bored at meetings and tends to doodle on his napkin. He occasionally gets interested in a project, but it takes some effort and has to involve him personally. He's nice and wouldn't hurt a flea. Don't expect him to lead the team, but he will do what you ask him to do. Put him on a team with a strong leader.

5. **Fighter:** Picks a fight with anyone for any reason. Loves debate and a good boxing round with others. You might wonder at times whether he's on your side or not, and he certainly can be exhausting, but his heart is in the right place. The fights can be unnecessary at times, but they aren't ill-intentioned. He is a good team player if you can keep him fighting against the competition instead of his teammates. Also needs a strong leader to channel his energies.

THE DESTRUCTIVE TYPES: These types will slow or stop any constructive goal. They waste time and energy and upset others.

1. **Angry**: He's always irritated about something, but won't always mention it. When things blow up, he's in the middle of it, yelling and screaming, throwing staplers and verbally abusing others. The accusations are untrue and full of destructive talk. The difference between "Angry" and "Fighter" is that the "Fighter" is fighting for something important: results. The Angry is just interested in beating others up. He's not trying to motivate them or prove his strategy is the best. He's just angry and obnoxious.

2. **Snake**: Also known as the gossip of the office, this 'type' is the mark of death for your office. Wanders from office to office, making seemingly harmless comments about others but secretly stirring up conflicts and problems. Casually "mentions" to the boss that Sheila was at lunch for 1.5 hours and smelled "a bit like alcohol" when she returned. Will profess to be doing every action for the good of others while casually inserting a knife into every back he or she can find. Will undermine every possible constructive goal. Will support and help destructive goals like layoffs or downsizing only. It's nearly guaranteed that you have met one of this type, but you might have missed it. The best skill you can learn is to recognize it when you see it. The snake is intensely dangerous while appearing completely harmless or even "nice" at times, and can be quite good at hiding his treachery by apparently "sensible" arguments and heavy doses of flattery. Look for a person who can't do an honest day's work and would rather sit around "talking" about problems and excuses rather than just driving the results. Will cause confusion to all constructive types in a short period of time. Get this person off the team if possible. If not, call a coach immediately.

3. **Afraid**: She's worried. She can't sleep. She needs another cup of coffee. The competition just sold the contract to the client! The sky is falling! She is the constantly worried officemate who has you wondering if you will ever get ahead or how so much can go so wrong so quickly. She is the bearer of bad tidings, and no good for you either. The world is much more dangerous place after you finish a breakfast meeting with her.

4. **Victim**: He just got in an accident. Again. He lost the sales contracts just before the big meeting because someone stole his briefcase at Starbucks. People are always stopping him, beating him up, picking on him. He can't win. Ever. You wonder how one person could have so much trouble and bad luck, and how he could miss so much work and still have a job. A popular type to start frivolous lawsuits. Stay away or you will be part of one of the lawsuits shortly. Don't hire him or you will have more and more problems on your hands daily.

5. **Sad**: She cries at the drop of a hat. She's a bit slow. She looks sad or blank most of the time. May be still stuck in a recent tragedy or just generally sad and depressed. Seems a little "out of it" at times. Hard to get moving toward goals. Points out what is wrong or bad about nearly everything. Not a good team player or even an individual contributor. Too slow and too many excuses to be useful.

6. **Apathetic**: He usually barely speaks. When he does, it is about how much he doesn't care, how it all is fruitless and a waste of time because failure is clearly right around the corner. Can't ever be convinced that something will go the right way. Has few friends. Doesn't move much or control much. His response to anything—either good or bad—could be summed up as, "Whatever".

So perhaps you found your teammates in the types, and perhaps you even discovered that one person was not as constructive as you might have hoped. It's time to get down to the most difficult question of the day: Are the few people you work with most often going to take YOU up with them? When they become successful, will you be successful too? Looking at these types should help you determine the answer to that question. The constructive types will, to a greater or lesser degree, help you, support you and work constructively toward the group goals. The destructive types won't. It's that simple. So take a good, long look at those around you and see what your group looks like.

Key point: High-performing teams consist of constructive team players.

Interpersonal Skills–continued

Part Two

------◆------

Deadly Gossip

Ever wondered how an office or a business could become so stressful? An insidious enemy, gossip can easily destroy a reputation or business. Learn how to spot hidden gossip and begin to eradicate it.

Recently, a mid-sized company nearly reached the brink of destruction in a flurry of scandal. The legal team swooped in and started swinging, taking out the major offenders but also cutting off 25% of the company's clients. Just before it spiraled completely out of control, a savvy board member spotted the exact problem and halted it. The culprit? A vicious round of gossip about the executive team followed by a lawsuit based on that gossip.

Gossip reaches as high as the C-suite and as low as the lunch room in nearly every company. It can seem harmless and inconsequential and even fun or interesting at times, but its roots can be deep and insidious. Perhaps you have seen a beneficial program cut because of gossip, or a contract lost or a person fired. Perhaps that person was you.

What can you do to proof yourself and your business against gossip? Education is the key. Gossip is so ingrained in our culture that sometimes we can miss gossip even when it is right in front of our faces. Gossip is defined as light conversation about sensational or private matters. The danger is the viral nature of this destructive and often untrue communication.

Here are a few pointers to recognize and control gossip.

1. Look for a broad generality.

"All the women around here are lazy," or "The marketing people are cold and calculating." This might seem to be obviously untrue upon inspection, but it can easily wend its way into conversations and become a stuck idea about the group. In the example above (a real one) about the marketing people, the result was that many people in the company avoided the "marketing people". This resulted in poor communications between sales and marketing, and a problem when it came to messaging the product. Not a good result. Pay attention whenever someone lays out a "truism" about an entire group. It's almost guaranteed to be a falsehood.

2. Check for negativity.

Very often, negative statements are largely or partially untrue, particularly if the statement is about a person's character or skills. These "opinions" which have no basis in fact can be very damaging. Call others on it when they throw them around as truth. Ex. "Tim is like a porcupine. Don't give him any new ideas. He just bristles." Not only is this likely false, but it creates problems for Tim. If you pass it along, you are an accomplice to wrecking Tim's relationships.

3. Look for "frequent liars".

"Frequent liars" are those who are routinely gossiping about others. Avoid them. Politely excuse yourself from the conversation. Why? Because **if they are gossiping to YOU about others, they will gossip to others about YOU as readily.** Don't get caught in the trap. Keep the conversation light and positive if you simply can't get away.

4. Inspect long-standing conflicts.

In any long-standing argument or conflict, there is certain to be a degree of gossip behind it. Get the two arguing parties together in a room and ask them this question: "Who says negative things to you about [the other person]?" Often, the same person is giving negative information to both sides! As soon as they both see what is happening, the conflict vanishes. Make sure you get a few names of people who were stirring up the conflict and work with those people to reduce their gossip level. This is fantastically useful in teambuilding.

Not all those who gossip have bad intentions. It is easy to get caught in a web of gossip in almost any workplace. Little by little, start educating others about the dangers of gossip and you will make your business and your life a little easier.

Truthfully, as an executive, you have no right to ever be caught gossiping. If you are unclear about how your perfect your behavior should be as an executive, read the Dale Carnegie book *How to Win Friends and Influence People*. It gives an excellent overview of the strong character an executive should possess.

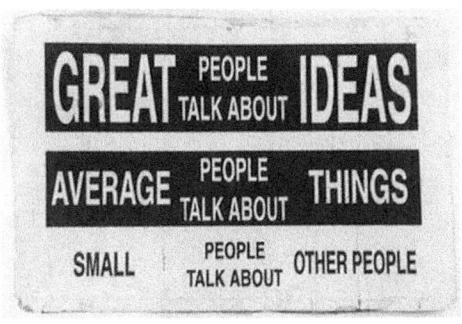

GREAT PEOPLE TALK ABOUT IDEAS

AVERAGE PEOPLE TALK ABOUT THINGS

SMALL PEOPLE TALK ABOUT OTHER PEOPLE

Key point: Don't gossip or allow gossip in your organization.

Delegation

Let Her Do Her Job

If you have any hope for sanity in running your team, read this chapter and implement it. If you want to continue to be overworked, underpaid and resentful of those who work for you who sneak out the door at 5:01 pm while you burn the midnight oil, then ignore this message at your peril.

There is one cause and ONLY one cause of overwork in an executive. Before revealing what that one cause is, we will first define executive. An EXECUTIVE is one *who gets others to get the work completed*. The root of the word "executive" is from the words for "follow through completely". So an executive in an organization is the one who is making sure the organization is running effectively by getting others to get the work done. If this is you, then it will behoove you to know the reason why you are overworked.

The root cause of overwork in an executive is doing the work of others! Do not fall into this trap. An organization cannot expand if an executive is acting as an individual contributor. You would be amazed at the number of ways executives invent to impede others from doing their jobs. Sometimes the intention of the executive is to "help" the person, but he ends up getting in the way. Read the examples below to see if they seem familiar to you:

1. The executive asks someone to complete a task, then interrupts and changes the task to be done.

   Example:
   Executive: "Bob, go research the market for bicycles."
   Bob does.
   Executive: "Bob, we need you to find out about the market for mopeds. I need it by Thursday."
   Bob: "So, don't do the bicycle research?"
   Executive: "No! I need the moped market research! Try to keep up!"

2. The executive does the job of the person for him.

   Example #1:
   Executive: "Bob, go research the market for bicycles."
   Bob does.
   Executive: "Bob, let me see what you are doing there. No, no, no, let me show you. You actually have to prepare the data first, then scrub the data. Move over and let me sit at your computer and show you."

   Example #2:
   Executive: "Bob, go research the market for bicycles."
   Bob does. The Executive, up at midnight, seeing no email that day from Bob, starts researching himself. When Bob comes in to present his data, the executive has already done the work and dismisses Bob.

3. The executive tells three (or five or seven) people to do the same task "just to make sure".

   Example:
   Executive: "Bob, go research the market for bicycles."
   Executive: "Jim, I need some research done on the market for bicycles."

Executive: "Janet, can you make sure that Bob is researching bicycles?"

Every example above results in two things. The first is an overworked executive and the second is an apathetic and irritated employee. Why? The executive ACTUALLY is not doing his own job which is to get **others** to get the work done. You fail as an executive to the degree that you fail to get others to get the work done.

You are very sharp if you are now asking yourself how you motivate your employees to do their jobs correctly. These are the key skills of an executive: motivation, influence, communication, follow-through and drive for results. You will see immediately that perhaps you could use some work in these areas. Most of us could.

Here are few short tips:

1. *Hire people with past production records.* This means past production on a resume is more important than personality or length of experience. You want to know that person has produced what you want him to produce in the past. Then you have a good chance the person will be able to get things done at your company.

2. *Train people well and often.* With no training plan or continuing education, you will have a hard time keeping people happy and keeping people at all. A competent person feels stable and stays in an organization. Unstable, unproductive people are unhappy and leave. An executive once told us he didn't have time to send his people to training. He had a sky-high turnover rate. He was barking up the wrong tree.

3. *Set clear expectations.* Explain exactly what you expect and when you expect it by. Otherwise, you will easily fall into one of the examples above.

4. ***Follow through appropriately.*** If a person is not doing his or her job at all, it is appropriate to get into the weeds and do his job for him/her. This should be a very temporary solution for a very unusual situation. If this is happening constantly, get a new person in the role. For the majority of the time, you as the executive should follow through by helping the person to overcome his own barriers. Don't solve it for him, but help him talk through how HE could solve it. Then send him off with his own solution, not yours. In this way, you are teaching him to independently solve problems.

5. ***Don't accept negative messages.*** Do not accept communication which states how something cannot be done or which complains about doing it. Get the person trained, productive and solving his own problems.

In summary, as difficult as it may sound, there is no hope for your schedule and the bags under your eyes unless you get others in the organization doing their work. If you continue to run areas or tasks for them, you will continue to be overworked and underpaid and you will burn out like a cheap firework. There is hope. You can help your organization. Get them doing their jobs competently and everyone wins.

Key point: Delegation is an essential skill for company and personal growth.

Influence

Part One

———◆———

Winning the Game of Office Politics

As you sit at your computer answering endless emails, the guy in the next cubicle just got promoted over you. Surprised? Look up from your inbox long enough to read this and you might win the next promotion.

Have you ever wondered how and why certain people made it to leadership positions? Did you ever wish you knew the magic ingredients that separate the average team member from the next VP? It's a little-known fact that office politics are a game you can win. The problem is that the rules are as unknown to most of us as the rules of dating. The so-called "rules" are tacit agreements made over the course of almost a century of office activity and human interaction and never before written down. Although all the "rules" might make for a separate book, this brief summary should give you a leg up over your colleagues and at least make you a bit more confident in your office dealings.

Rule #1: Yes, it IS about WHO you know.

You probably are not surprised about this, but you may be asking yourself how you make inroads without obviously sucking up. Well, the answer might surprise you. There are two roads to power in the game of influence. The first is to know all the right people, the most influential and powerful of your circle. The second, however, is to know the largest amount of people. That's right, it's a numbers game. This means your lines of communication have to go WAY out, both internally and externally. As an example, what if during the next leadership team meeting, your name is spoken in glowing terms, *not by your boss,* but by an executive from another division? Your boss gets congratulations for your good work. Certainly you can see how you might rise quickly in your boss' estimation. So, when looking at WHO to schmooze, don't just consider the obvious power sources, but consider ones outside your normal sphere. Play pick-up basketball with the head of the marketing division. Invite the approachable Senior Director in IT to your next presentation and get her feedback. The easiest way to get a handle on who you could start to influence is to map out all the people you know in your surrounding areas.

Tip: Make an influence map. Put your name in the middle of a blank page. On the right of the page, list out all the people you know well and put connecting lines between yourself and each of them. On the left side of the page, put a list of people you would like to know and put dotted lines to each of them. Now, your task over the coming months is to move people from the left to the right. Or, if you like, you can simply darken the dotted line each time a connection is made. Eventually, your paper should be full of names and lines, showing a larger circle of influence for you. This tactic works even if you are in a small company. Simply include many external contacts, like customers and business partners. After you have your list, be certain to include a ranking of who is most positive or friendly, as they are always the easiest to get to know. Look for people who are "connectors", those who will introduce you to other people as well. This gets you more bang for your networking buck.

Rule #2: Man cannot live on work alone.

So many people live under the myth (or dangerous assumption) that if they do good work, they will be rewarded. Sadly, this is not true. You may be the best at what you do, but if no one knows about it, it won't impact your career. All the good work in the world will go down the drain without a little *Personal Public Relations. Personal Public Relations* is very simply getting your (great) work well-known. No, you don't have to hire an agent, but you do have to be aware of how you are perceived by others. If you are one of those nose-to-the-grindstone sorts, your perception in the organization might be ***non-existent.*** To solve this problem, simply begin to establish commonalities with others in your organization. Be a little more communicative. Send a few more emails that are "informational" about your work. Loop in five times as many people about what you are doing. Ask for ways to become more visible, like presentations. It's common marketing knowledge that a potential customer has to see your message nine to 27 times before they buy! Use this concept if you want to be known in your office and start by communicating more and more frequently. This is particularly important for you if your upper layer of management is remote. You simply MUST find ways to get in front of the next layer up in the chain of command. Use whatever means possible to keep the communication flowing.

Tip: So you are shy. You don't want to communicate more. You don't like this whole idea of *Personal Public Relations.* Don't worry. Start with a method of communication that you are comfortable with, such as email. Send a few more emails than you normally would. Or, if you like one-on-one conversations rather than group discussions, work out how you can drop by a few people's offices and check in. Take a prepared topic to discuss and make it short. Just let them see your face a little. Remember, it's a numbers game. Imagine each communication you gave was a little hash mark on your score sheet. Try to get many hash marks in a day.

If all of this is sounding a bit like tooting your own horn, and you don't like the sound of that horn, then you have just spotted one of your own barriers to success. If you think talking about what you have done and getting others to recognize it is some sort of harmful action, you are going to have a rough time getting the word out. If you feel this way, don't worry. Take it slowly and do a little bit at a time. A few more connections is better than none, so pat yourself on the back when you make any improvement at all. And keep going.

Key point: Hard work is important but must be bolstered by communication to get attention.

Influence

Part Two

Handle Fear in Others

Perhaps you would like to wield some influence in your organization. You want someone to believe you, follow your plan, take your suggestion, promote you. You have to convince him that you are right, that he should listen to you. The first thing you need to know is how he is going to react to you. There is one fundamental human reaction to **all** attempts to persuade, sell or influence. It is FEAR.

Any person you are talking to can easily become afraid the moment you try to influence him. Why? He is afraid of failing or making a mistake or buying the wrong product or getting ripped off. He has been burned before and vowed not to let it happen again. The more experienced the person, the more likely you are to encounter these fear reactions. You are dealing with an intelligent person who intends to make good decisions, and he has promised himself not to make poor decisions. So, as you start to persuade, he develops anxiety, agitation and apprehension about the pitch. He wraps himself in a "brick coat" to defend himself. The coat is made up of all the arguments you must overcome to persuade him.

The good news is that these fear reactions follow a predictable pattern:

1. **Prevention.** As soon as you have described your purpose in talking to him, the **first set** of reactions are called "prevention" or "inhibition" reactions. These reactions add time, prevent or prohibit your actions from happening. He is trying to hold you off, stop you, prevent you. "Let's talk next week." "I need to check with my wife." "I'm not sure I have enough information; I'll have my associate start some due diligence for us." These are all prevention reactions. The most common of these is the "delay" reaction.

   As the persuader, you need to know that the biggest enemy you have is time. The more time he adds, the more likely he is to say no. Just know that these delay tactics are simply irrational fears and proceed with the conversation. Do not allow the person to "think about it" (thinking doesn't actually take any time) or to take time off from the conversation. Just keep pushing ahead. While he wants time to work against you, you need to make it work for you by staying interested. Remember to be kind, non-argumentative, and continually interested in moving the discussion forward. Keep a cool head. Don't get too attached to the outcome, but be more interested in hearing his point of view fully.

2. **Argument.** The next fear reaction is a bit tougher to take. In fact, this reaction stops most influencers in their tracks. Most people would rather light their own eyebrows on fire than confront the potential conflict that may occur in this phase. Time to toughen up your courage. The person you are trying to influence just might get a bit angry or

frustrated that you called his bluff. He might yell or call you names at the extreme end. Don't worry; you have simply arrived at the second fear stage. Congratulate yourself (silently) and proceed. Despite all the reasons and objections and arguments and doubts he expresses, just know they are all based in fear. Confidently and calmly, WITH AS MUCH ADMIRATION as you can muster, continue to reassure him of you and your idea or plan. Stay upbeat and positive and INTEREST him in it by being interested in him and his ideas about whatever you are discussing. If you can push through these fear reactions, he will eventually move through the fear and doubts and upsets.

3. **Reversal.** The strangest thing will happen if you push through the argument phase. He will begin to reverse his decision and start to agree with you. Your job in this phase is to be quiet and let him talk himself into your point of view. And, if you continue to be interested and have remained kindly persistent you will arrive at the final phase. Finally, the fear is dissipating.

4. **Interest.** Your confidence and positive energy and INTEREST will win the day and he will agree with you and take action. The best part is that you have both won. You used your impeccable influence skills and he made the right choice. It's a win-win situation.

Key point: Most people react to influence with some fear, but the fear can be dissolved.

Influence

Part Three

The Power of Four

A CTO of a large company called me in frustration one day because he could not convince his senior management team to relieve the technical debt on their website. **Technical debt** means old, outdated or unworkable coding that makes for more work for the developers down the road. It is equivalent to rigging your plumbing up with duct tape and wire and hoping it lasts 30 years. He wanted to clean up the back end of the site to make sure that going forward the site would be workable and efficient as they added new features. This was a wise strategy, but the senior management team could not see the benefit. They truly did not understand why he would prioritize this over getting a new feature ready right away and they missed how the trade-offs would work. And actually, some of the engineers didn't find this work particularly glamorous either so they refused to help him persuade anyone. It seemed the whole organization was against him.

Here are the four steps this CTO used to get the senior management team to invest in handling the technical debt.

1. **Stop all debate**. The CTO had been very busy "making his case" with all the other executives, pretending he was a lawyer trying to win in a courtroom. I cannot stress enough how *ineffective* this is as a technique. Your colleagues do not want to face up to an opposing lawyer on their typical Tuesday. They wake up, have their coffee and head to work hoping to have a pleasant day, not to meet Perry Mason in the hallway, giving them a list of reasons why they are wrong. If you are currently using this technique with your colleagues, please reconsider. 99.99% of people do not want to be wrong and will fight with you just to prove they are not, despite all evidence to the contrary. As soon as you set yourself up as "opposing counsel" you have lost. You must take your issue out of the realm of debate. Never criticize them, condemn them or complain they "don't get it". This increases the feeling that you are telling them they are wrong and they will become more and more defensive, no matter how irrational it may seem.

2. **Seek understanding.** Instead, ask your colleagues about their perspectives. Spend time attempting to understand why they view the situation the way they do. You will discover a few pieces of education about your topic they are missing. Do not yet try to remedy this! Just listen attentively and truly understand their points. When you feel you have a full understanding, acknowledge them sincerely (with words like, "I see what you are saying.") and then thank them for their time. Do not attempt to get your point across at this moment. Instead, build agreement. Find areas where you agree with the person completely and acknowledge those first. Make it your business to truly understand the perspective of the other while making him feel comfortable that you are listening.

3. **Educate**. Next, if in your discussions you realized there are areas of missing education among the people you are trying to influence, spend the time to educate them. As you create a way to educate them, remember #2 and their perspective. Approach the education from their point of view, and be certain you are not arguing or criticizing as you educate. Bring facts and figures that show how your perspective is correct, but along the way, mention how you noticed their good points. Ex.: "When I talked to Sandra, she mentioned that we might not have enough engineering resources to create forward progress as well as handle technical debt. This is a good point she made. Here is a potential way we could handle this problem." In your education, handle the actual concerns your colleagues could have because you understand those concerns fully now.

4. **Be gracious**. All the way along, and especially as you make your case, be gracious and friendly. Continually thank others (genuinely) for any contributions they made and for any input they gave. This gives you the appearance of considering the whole business, not just your area, and others will now consider you a team player.

These four steps of influence build trust over time. The first time you use these steps, others may not yet trust you, but as you use it continually, you will find more and more that they like working with you and no longer shun you in the hallway. They are much more likely to talk to you, a friend and colleague, than you as Perry Mason. Soon, they will begin working for your causes, helping you get your points across. And as you return the favor for them, you can get more persuasion done in less time than you ever imagined.

Key point: Influence is one of the most important and misunderstood skills in any business context. Learn it well and you will create success for yourself and others.

Communication

Part One

Shoot the Messenger!

n fact, fire him. While these words might seem harsh, you just
might save your team by doing so. Read on.

Recently, I got a puzzling call from one of my favorite HR
directors asking me what he should do with a group of engineers who just could not get along. The company's product
was behind because the engineers were arguing so much that
they could not get any work done. One of the engineers worked
from home because he refused to come in to the office. He was
considering a "hostile workplace" claim. I dug into the situation
and asked questions, but a particular question was incredibly
revealing: "Who tells you about all the problems between the
engineers?"

We all have to pass on bad news now and then. Most of us
do not enjoy it. But a few people thrive on it. Call them drama
queens, pot-stirrers or gossip-mongers, but no matter the name,

they tend to follow the same pattern. The pattern, from your perspective, will look like this:

1. A person enters your office or cubicle and mentions some bad news. Possibly even asks you to check it out.

2. You go to investigate the scene or take it up with the other party.

3. You find the other party just as upset as you are and it certainly looks like something went wrong. You note that this is a dysfunctional person or group. You may even develop a slight headache.

What happened behind the scenes was your so-called "messenger" went to the other party first and told him something equally horrifying. Now you are all trying to figure out a situation sown with lies and exaggerations. Confusion, conflict and upset are the goals of the messenger.

It is possible you do not want to believe such "messengers of doom" exist. But they do. Here are a few ways to detect those who quietly stir the pot:

1. The "messengers of doom" show no remorse in telling you how bad people or situations are. The vast majority of people do not like to mention that something or someone is bad, but these messengers do not hesitate to pass on the bad news. The usual lines are that someone is (or you are) in trouble or in danger and they give an exaggerated view of how bad it is.

2. Such people also love gossip, critical remarks or any state-ment which reduces the reputation of others. "JoAnn said you were the worst bookkeeper she's ever worked with. Can you believe she said that?" The criticisms often come in streams and can be about multiple people. The favorite

tactic is to spread what others supposedly said about you. Note that it is very likely untrue or altered in some way.

3. These messengers often stir up conflict between two people intentionally. If you see two people fighting relentlessly, ask each person who else has told them bad things about the other. You might find both people have heard from 'the messenger'.

4. Usually, the "messengers of doom" go about their business quietly. They do not shout from the rooftops; they slink casually into offices, close the door and gossip. Or they slide up to you while you type and say, "Did you hear that . . ."

5. "Messengers of doom" can be intelligent or dull, in high or low places. When in executive roles, they will often gravitate toward the most productive or creative areas and try to create conflict there.

Why do the "messengers of doom" behave this way? Basically, there are two tendencies in any person. One tendency is to do well and succeed. The other tendency is to give up or give in or destroy things. The "messengers of doom" have stronger negative tendencies than they do positive ones. While this is a subject of great curiosity, the more important point is to recognize it when you see it. The easiest way to start your investigation for "messengers of doom" in your office is to ask yourself who brings you the most bad news and criticism. Then, before you do anything else, look for other patterns of gossip and criticism from that person. Just pay attention, ask questions and observe. The next step is to go to HR or someone who can help with the situation.

Back to our engineers. As it happens, the "messenger of doom" was one of the engineers who was planting gossip about the other engineers all over the group. He was so busy at it that his own work was suffering. Once he was detected and watched, it became quite obvious that he was creating conflicts between the other engineers. He was fired a week later and now the group harmoniously codes away. The engineer who worked from home comes in four days a week.

If your office has too much conflict or you get stressed or tired from dealing with others in your group, start to look for an "MD". Maybe you need to shoot the messenger*.

*Warning: "shoot" is a figurative term!

Key point: Executives should receive good news more often than bad.

Communication

Part Two

———◆———

Don't Take That Message

arrived in the office yesterday morning to the following message on my desk: "Company X cancelled the project. Thanks." What a depressing way to start the day. Turns out, it was not even true. Company X had simply called to move the start date and wanted some information about how to change the contract. I could say no one is to blame for this poor communication or for Company X wanting to change something. Or I could assume it was a simple mistake. I am a bit more demanding. I prefer to look at the bigger picture on what types of communication I should accept and, in fact, demand, of those who communicate with me.

Executives are juggling many tasks daily. In truth, we do not have time for mistaken or upsetting communication. It drags down our morale and wastes precious time to clarify the situation. Stacked up over and over, it can cripple our businesses.

What if we only accepted certain types of communication? What if we demanded people communicate with us in better, more concise, more positive ways? It's a new view on time and energy management.

Businesses are made of flows of communication. We put out marketing and sales efforts (output) and we get in customer calls or sales (input). Then we send out services and get in money in return. These input-output patterns are like the breathing of our businesses.

Extending this "breathing" analogy, no one would want to be placed in a room of poisonous gas and be asked to breathe. If the communications you receive and give in a day are all negative, then your businesses are "breathing" toxicity.

If you want to have your business breathing "clean air" via clean communications, only accept communications that provide:

a) valid information;
b) requests for authorization of well thought-out proposals;
c) confirmation that something got done; or
d) good news.

Next, go even further and reject communications that
a) demand you make a decision about some issue that you know very little about;
b) give reasons why something cannot be accomplished; or
c) relay constant bad news.

In feudal days, kings would behead messengers who constantly brought bad news. While I don't recommend beheading, try to imagine your day free of those negative communications. Sound idyllic? While it might take a little work and a little re-training of your colleagues, it can be done. We teach people how to treat us.

Here are the four simple steps to implement this plan in your office:

1. Inform those with whom you communicate most fre-quently of your new "good news, solutions and informa-tion" policy. Use the paragraph above to show them the types of communications you expect and give short exam-ples of each.

2. If you get an incorrect communication like the one in my example at the beginning of the article, send it back with a short, polite note to the writer. Example: "Sue, thank you for this note. I am unclear what happened here. Please rewrite this message explaining exactly what happened and a possible solution. I appreciate it!"

3. Watch your mood improve. You are in control and your office is already more positive.

4. Share this plan with other executives who can also improve their situations and start communicating correctly to you.

Key point: Communication is the lifeblood of an organization. Keep it flowing and clean.

Executive Presence

M any executive presence skills are also covered under interpersonal relationships and influence. This is also a vast topic to be covered more thoroughly in future editions. This chapter is designed mainly to dispel a major misconception about leadership and which harms the executive presence of so many.

Toughness

I was wrong about something. I know, I am as shocked as you are. The only reason I am willing to share it is that it might help you to know it. Otherwise, I would still pretend I was right.

It all began in a blustery autumn about 10 years ago. I was coaching attorneys, doctors and other executives, and I was interested in understanding the traits of leadership. I had some natural leaders in the bunch and I was watching them and their behavior to see how they ran their offices and lives. I watched them give feedback, make project plans, and push for results. I did not use the scientific method, admittedly, but I started to shape some ideas about what made certain leaders stand out.

I formulated a hypothesis that good leaders were tough, meaning they were tenacious, hard-edged, persistent, and definitely on the unsympathetic side. Natural leaders who could get work done were hard on their people. Yes, it was all coming together. There was a study released about the same time which showed that a "drive for results" was the most important determining factor in executive success. Drive is the operative word, right? I was getting somewhere. These are the "doers" in life, and if they have to take a few people out along the way, so be it. These natural leaders knew how to rant, stomp their feet, jump up and down, and GET RESULTS! Some of them were underhanded, sly, even a bit vicious, but I could never argue with those results.

I kept this viewpoint for a long time, coaching many people to be tough, to give difficult feedback with pitiless precision, to attack weak points in the organization with ardor. It worked to a great degree. Tough executives made names for themselves and sent their companies' results UPWARD consistently.

In the spring of 2009, after the economy was in full collapse, I noticed something that shook my stable data about executive competencies. These drivers, these "tough" executives were uniformly looking for work. Nearly all of them had been let go in the downturn. They were a bit friendless. Interestingly, some others who had not taken the "toughness" route and had worked on other competencies were still around. I realized it might be time to reinvent my coaching style.

I started to take a different look at executives at that time. I dug into an objective look at the executives who survived the downturn, and I want to announce a new hypothesis. *Executives who are tough with results but kind with people succeed longer and more often.* Yes, I said it. Kindness matters.

A recent example gives us window into this. A CEO of a mid-sized company was down-sizing his company recently, and he started to lose his hair rather rapidly. I asked him one day what was stressing him so badly and he commented that firing people took an enormous toll. He never did stop thinking about how it affected the families and lives of those who had left. He was having trouble sleeping, and had seen his doctor for several stress tests. There was nothing physically wrong with him, but he looked and felt old and tired.

I decided to try an experiment with him and ask him to take several kind actions per week as his work allowed. I had him make a list of small kindnesses he could do that would have an impact on his workplace morale. One of his items was to institute a bagel breakfast for the administrative staff every other Friday. He paid for the bagels personally to keep the company budget stable. Then he made a point of complimenting the good work of his assistant on a more frequent basis. He listed 15 separate kind actions he could take over the coming months. Curiously, his hair stopped falling out. Even more curiously, his company started doing better too. A statistician could argue that the correlation is meaningless. That is fine by me. This is not a mathematical argument so much as a statement from the heart. My experiment in kindness made a difference for everyone involved.

Perhaps you know an executive who is suffering personally for his own lack of kindness. He is not only hurting himself, but he is hurting his company. Being too "tough", not having enough kindness, is no sign of strength. It is just a contributor to stress. The times we suffer most are the times we could have been just a bit nicer and wonder why were weren't.

After all, we could all agree the last economic downturn was not easy on anyone. We all had it rough. Consider this the next time you have a choice to make: what is the kind thing to do? The kind choice might just bring a smile to your face as well as the face of the person on the other end. After all, what are we doing here in this world anyway? Are we here to make it a miserable experience for others? Must we be hectic, texting-and-driving maniacs who only care about the next dollar? Are 10 more pallets delivered more important than the life and dignity of our fellow colleagues? It is about time we got our priorities straight. Get results, certainly. Push hard for them. Hold high standards for your people. But hold them with kindness too. You might find it gets you further than you think.

Key point: A tough executive can also be kind.

Prologue

———————

I chose the tools in this book because they were the most pressing topics on the minds of business people I encountered. And they fit with the topics that came up most often on our 360 reviews. They are not, however, all the tools that exist. Feel free to email me (jill@becoachable.com) and suggest other topics that would help you, and I will compile them into the second edition or a future book.

I truly hope the tools in this book are useful to you. I hope you enjoy using them as much as I have enjoyed my 12 years of coaching executives. I have found people in business in America to be some of the most hard-working, tenacious, upright and personable people I could have imagined. The businesses of America are the reasons why we have one of the strongest economies in the world. And no matter what international politics does to our country, we are still one of the most productive and creative nations in the world. It has been my privilege to work with some of the brightest minds in our country and to help them with some of their most complicated problems. I feel honored to have helped them along the road in some way. I hope that as you use these tools, you use them in the spirit they were intended, the spirit of goodwill and help for our colleagues who are the building blocks of our country.

With admiration,

Jill Chiappe

jill@becoachable.com

www.BeCoachable.com

About the Author

Jill Chiappe interviews and coaches top-level executives for 360° assessments and leadership development programs. She also trains small executive teams to become high-functioning teams. She has trained multiple hundreds of leadership team members on key topics such as handling conflicts, increasing production and streamlining teamwork. Jill's seminars are often the highest-rated in her client companies.

Jill founded and runs Coachability, Inc. (www.BeCoachable.com) a coaching practice which began in San Diego, California in 2000. Jill's clients have included executives from Fortune 100 companies such as **Cisco, Gap, Inc., Amgen**, **Google** and **Dell**, as well as dozens of venture-funded Silicon Valley start-ups.

Jill is a member of Women's Economic Ventures in Ventura County and recently won the Women's Economic Ventures

"Bloomers" award for the most successful woman-owned business. Jill also writes regular articles for many business and executive networking venues, such as the Santa Barbara Human Resources Association and Biznik of Los Angeles. Jill's articles have been published in numerous Human Resources trade journals.

Most of all, Jill truly enjoys coaching executives and she wins every time they win.

www.ingramcontent.com/pod-product-compliance
Lightning Source LLC
Chambersburg PA
CBHW051343170526
45166CB00002B/940